PHASES OF
CREATION

For My Parents

Louis and Evelyn Goldstein

ISBN: 13: 978-0692313695
ISBN: 10: 0692313699

Phases Of Creation
Sheila R. Vitale

Requests for permission to reproduce selections
from this book should be mailed to:

Living Epistles Ministries
Sheila R. Vitale
P O Box 562
Port Jefferson Station, NY 11776-0562 USA
(631) 331-1493

Living Epistles Ministries

Sheila R. Vitale

Pastor, Teacher, Founder

PO Box 562

Port Jefferson Station, NY 11776 USA

PHASES OF CREATION

Edited and Adapted as a Book by
Sheila R. Vitale

PHASES OF CREATION

Was Transcribed and Edited for Clarity, Continuity of Thought, and
Punctuation by

The *LEM* Transcribing and Editing Team

Living Epistles Ministries
~ Judeo-Christian Spiritual Philosophy ~
Sheila R. Vitale
Pastor, Teacher & Founder

Ministry Staff
Anthony Milton, Teacher (South Carolina)
Brooke Paige, Teacher (New York)
Sandra Aldrich (MN) (July 7, 1975 – April 18, 2021)

Administrative Staff
Susan Panebianco, Office Manager

Editorial Staff
Rose Herczeg, Editor

Technical Staff
Lape Mobolaji-Lawal, Database Administrator

Ministry Illustrators
Cecilia H. Bryant (Oct. 18, 1921 – Oct. 23, 2013)
Fidelis Onwubueke

Music Staff
June Eble, Singer, Lyricist and Clarinetist
(July 20, 1931 – Jan. 24, 2024)
Don Gervais, Singer, Lyricist and Guitarist
Rita L. Rora, Singer, Lyricist and Guitarist

Table of Contents

The Alternate Translation Bible©

The Alternate Translation Bible (**ATB**) is an original translation of the Scripture.

Alternate Translation of the Old Testament©
Alternate Translation, Exodus, Chapter 32
    (Crime of the Calf)©
Alternate Translation, Daniel, Chapter 8©
Alternate Translation, Daniel, Chapter 11©

Alternate Translation of the New Testament©
Alternate Translation, 2 Thessalonians, Chapter 2
    (Sophia)©
Alternate Translation, 1st John, Chapter 5©
Alternate Translation, the Book of Colossians
    (To The Church At Colosse) ©
Alternate Translation, the Book of Corinthians, Chapter 11
    (Corinthian Confusion) ©
Alternate Translation, the Book of Jude
    (The Common Salvation)©

Alternate Translation of the Book of the Revelation of Jesus Christ to
    St. John©
Traducción Alternada del Libro de Revelación de Jesucristo©

I.

IN THE BEGINNING

In the beginning there were waters and Jehovah's seed. The waters in the abyss (also called *the pit* and *Sheol*) are spiritual energy. They are not the waters of this world. Neither is Jehovah's seed a simple particle. It consists of trillions of photons, spiritual particles of light.

The energized waters in the abyss are called *Elohim*.

Jehovah's single light seed is called *Michael and his mate*, because it has both a male and a female aspect.

Elohim from a higher world hovered over the energized waters in the abyss and spread the *light seed* of Jehovah's son upon the surface of the waters of the lower world.

The two Elohims, one from a higher world and the other from a lower world, can be likened to mother and daughter. They both are of the same substance, but the substance of Elohim in the higher world is called *Spirit* and is gaseous, and Elohim in the lower world is called *water*, and is liquid. Spiritual water is called *soul*.

Jehovah's light seed interacted with the lower Elohim's energized waters, and a spiritual by-product which can be likened to rust, emerged out of the side of Michael's mate, the female aspect of Jehovah's light seed. The Scripture calls it *earth; spiritual earth*.

Elohim, the energized waters of the abyss, and Jehovah's light seed, Michael and his mate, are collectively called *Jehovah's spiritual seminal fluid*.

1

Gen 1:2

> [2] AND THE EARTH WAS WITHOUT FORM, AND VOID; AND DARKNESS WAS UPON THE FACE OF THE DEEP. AND THE SPIRIT OF GOD MOVED UPON THE FACE OF THE WATERS. **KJV**

Everything that exists, including the galaxies and the stars of outer space, exists in the abyss.

The spiritual waters of Jehovah's seminal fluid are the energy of creation.

The created world is an image formed from the light seed bouncing off of the waters of creation. This world exists because the seed that is bouncing off of the waters of creation is the Serpent's seed.

When Adam's renewed seed, the seed of the Lord Jesus Christ, reflects off of the waters of creation, this world will change into the image of the Lord Jesus, the personality that veils Jehovah.

The image of God will be restored in the individual, one man at a time, and eventually, this world will be translated into another world. The creation will become gaseous again, and the solid physical body will dissolve, and we shall live forever.

II.

ADAM

The higher Elohim that spread Jehovah's seed upon the lower Elohim's energized waters, is called *the Spirit of Life*. The spiritual essence that undergirds all of creation is called *breath* in the high place where Jehovah and Elohim dwell, but that same essence is called *soul* in the field of creation. *Soul* is *spiritual water*.

The spiritual earth that emerged out of the female side of Jehovah's light seed remained attached to her, and was eventually formed into the first Adam.

The first Adam is made from the spiritual earth, but he also has a watery side, called soul. Adam exists in the water of the soul world, but he also stands out of the water, and can be seen in the dry parts of the earth.

Elohim and Michael and his mate, Jehovah's spiritual seminal fluid, are the River of Life that flows out of Eden, and Adam is the living plant that grows there.

Genesis 1:1 and Genesis 2:7 describe the same event on two parallel worlds.

Gen 1:1

¹ IN THE BEGINNING GOD CREATED THE HEAVEN AND THE EARTH. **KJV**

<u>Gen 2:7</u>

[7] AND THE LORD GOD FORMED MAN OF THE DUST OF THE GROUND, AND BREATHED INTO HIS NOSTRILS THE BREATH OF LIFE; AND MAN BECAME A LIVING SOUL. **KJV**

III.

THE WOMAN

Everything in God's Kingdom is male. The concept of *a female side* exists only as a function of the male. A Captain, for example, is male to a Lieutenant, and that same Lieutenant, who is female to the Captain, is male to the Sergeant. This concept is called *fluctuating spiritual sexual roles,* meaning, *relationships based on function, rather than on the form of the body.*

Functional sexuality depends on the relationship between individuals. For example, a wife is female to her husband, but male to her children.

The energized waters of Jehovah's spiritual seminal fluid carry Jehovah's life-giving seed. In our world, the sperm is the head of the water side of the seminal fluid, but everything is reversed in the Spirit, where Elohim's energized water is the head of the seed. The waters of creation are male to the female seed that is destined to produce Jehovah's son.

The female side of Jehovah's light seed completed herself by joining, as a male, to the female earth that was growing out of her side. This is how Michael and his mate, Jehovah's righteous light seed, was corrupted, and transformed into *Samael and his mate, the Serpent.*

Adam of the World of Creation is the singularity that contains Elohim's energized waters and Jehovah's light seed. The chain of authority within Adam of Creation is: Jehovah, Elohim, Seed. But Samael and his mate, the seed that transformed from Michael and his mate into Samael and his mate, overcame Elohim and

5

acquired his energized waters, which now serve Samael, rather than Jehovah.

Samael and his mate and Elohim are called ***the Woman***.

PHASES OF CREATION

IV.

LUCIFER

Lucifer is the name of the Woman's offspring. *Lucifer* means *light-bearer*. A Jesuit priest translated that Hebrew word that means *light-bearer*, as the name, *Lucifer,* the one who carries the light.

Lucifer, the Woman's illegitimate offspring, *carries her* in this material world, but they have utterly failed to provide immortal bodies to dwell in. Mankind continues to die from generation to generation, so new bodies must be provided for them continually.

Lucifer said, I shall be like Elohim (God). I shall also be like the Most High, and greater than He.

The significance of the Name, *the Most High*, is that it means *the ability to reproduce*. *The Most High* is a translation of *El Elyon*, *the high one above the high one,* who carries the DNA of an immortal creation. Lucifer, by calling himself *The Most High*, is saying that he, as well as Jehovah, has the power and authority to produce and sustain an immortal creation.

Lucifer is the man of sin, the offspring of the incestuous adultery of fallen Adam's internal parts. *Lucifer* is a pseudo male, the spiritual eunuch who said, *I will ascend above the stars, and I will be greater than God.*

V.

THE BETRAYAL

Jehovah warned Adam, the whole man, saying, ***Do not mix with the seed of the earth, because the earth is the Serpent's seed.*** Jehovah knew that if his virile seed joined with the Serpent's seed instead of the spiritual waters, the creature which was intended to be a civilized spiritual man in the image of Jehovah, would become the exact opposite: A savage animal in the form of a solid clay image.

So, Jehovah said to Adam, Keep the garden. The Hebrew word translated keep, means to militarily guard. Do not let yourself turn into a solid clay animal, because, if you do, Michael and his mate, my spiritual life within you will die.

Michael's female side is attached to Michael on one side, and the earth that grows out of her, on the other side. Michael and his mate are supposed to dominate and control the animal nature of the earth, but Michael's mate betrayed him and committed adultery with the earth that grows out of her side.

Adam, the creation of God, is a civilized spiritual man when Michael and his mate control Adam's animal side, but Michael's mate joined with the earth and began to dominate Michael, the male side of the Righteous Seed. This perverse, illegal relationship between Michael's mate and the animal nature of the earth changed Adam into a savage uncivilized man, and a corrupt, perverse world emerged as his environment -- the product of spiritual incest.

9

Elohim's substance is called *water* in our world, but in the World of Creation it is described as *gaseous*.

Before the Fall, the waters of creation mixed with the earth to form Adam's gaseous, spiritual body, and those spiritual waters ebbed and flowed like the ocean tides that are influenced by the moon. Likewise, Jehovah's virile seed exerted a form of inner spiritual gravity upon the gaseous body that maintained Adam's form.

After that, however, the earth illegally completed Michael's mate, and the adulterous couple enslaved Michael and forced Elohim's gaseous substance underground.

Gen 1:20

> [20] AND GOD SAID, LET THE WATERS BRING FORTH ABUNDANTLY THE MOVING CREATURE THAT HATH LIFE, AND FOWL THAT MAY FLY ABOVE THE EARTH IN THE OPEN FIRMAMENT OF HEAVEN. **KJV**

But, despite Jehovah's warning, the earth that Adam, the living plant, was growing out of seduced Adam, the head of all of his parts, and the earth within Adam mixed with Michael and his mate.

Jehovah's virile seed became a conscious clay animal that surrounded the waters of creation, and Elohim, the energy of creation, became a stagnant pool of putrefied water called *Satan*.

The creation is now solid, rather than watery or gaseous, because the water, or the energy, is trapped inside of us. It is land-locked, like a lake, rather than free-flowing like a river that empties into a sea.

Nevertheless, according to the Alternate Translation Bible, Jehovah continues to call Adam, the creation of God, his son, saying: The virile seed of my son is appearing as Leviathan, the pride of man, and his mate has become the intelligent animal consciousness of this fallen world.

VI.

THE FALLEN WORLD

Adam, Jehovah's Son, was forced into a female role, and today he is in complete submission to the female earth. For this reason, the Scripture calls fallen Adam a homosexual harlot.

Acts 17:6

> [6] AND WHEN THEY FOUND THEM NOT, THEY DREW JASON AND CERTAIN BRETHREN UNTO THE RULERS OF THE CITY, CRYING, THESE THAT HAVE TURNED THE WORLD UPSIDE DOWN ARE COME HITHER ALSO; **KJV**

This fallen world is upside down. Hindus know that this world is upside down and stand on their heads in an attempt to rectify the imbalance within themselves. It is the world inside of us that is upside down, not the world on the outside.

I have dreamed about people walking with their heads attached to the ceiling as if they were helium balloons, instead of with their feet on the ground.

We walk with our carnal mind, rather than with our righteous mind, and live out of the lusts of our emotions, rather than rational thought. Our mind must be turned around, but only Christ Jesus can do that for us. Christ Jesus, the last Adam, is now in charge of mankind, but only a few of us know about it. He is replacing the first Adam, who became a homosexual harlot.

Jehovah's seed contains the building blocks of creation, but life is only through union with Jehovah. Our world is conscious because of Jehovah's fallen seed, but it has no life because we are separated from the Living One. A world that is separated from

God is hell. There are degrees of hell. This visible world, right here where we live, is a degree of hell.

There are also degrees of pain in hell. Some people have more problems than others. It makes no difference if you are tortured by drug abuse, or as a prostitute controlled by a pimp, or if you are an outstanding citizen, or a prosperous professional. Even if you are wealthy, respected, and loved by the community, you are still in a state of death because you lack true Life, and the lack of true Life is hell. If you exist in this world, you are in one of the degrees of hell and, therefore, you must have some sort of pain or trouble in your life.

Job asked the Lord, Why did you do this to me? Why not tell me what I am doing wrong so that I can change? Jehovah answered Job, saying, You do not have the power to change.

Adversity convinces us that we cannot change ourselves. As soon as we realize that we need God to change us, we are on the road to victory.

Christ Jesus is the spiritual weapon by which we escape from hell. By his strength, we must wage a spiritual war against the enemies in our own mind.

Today, there is a false doctrine that says we cannot attain to that high spiritual place by ourselves as individuals; we must ascend as a corporate body. But the inquisition is hidden in this doctrine. It is dangerous to force people to be like you because you think you cannot get to heaven without them.

Variations of this wicked doctrine are widespread today, not only in the Church, but in the whole world! It teaches that doctrine is divisive, and must be put away, so that we can all ascend together. Once sound doctrine is removed, however, the false doctrine of tyranny will be forced on the people.

VII.

DECEPTION IN THE CHURCH

Several of the brethren and I attended a Pastors' conference in Connecticut recently, which was conducted by the head pastor at Pinecrest, a Christian Bible School which, at that time, had campuses at upstate New York and Long Island. Before we left for the conference, the Lord told me to prepare to sleep over **Karen's house**. This was an unusual command because I did not know anyone by that name. We did meet someone named Karen, and she did invite us to stay at her house overnight. We would not have attended the second day of the conference and would not have heard the message we were sent to hear without Karen's invitation.

We listened as the head pastor spoke about the supernatural move of the Spirit and the miracles that took place in a local church. He said that there was such a mighty move of the Spirit, that the pulpit broke in half, and that spiritual power has been flowing there ever since.

The head pastor continued to speak about the state of the Church, and I soon realized that there was much more going on than I had realized. The head pastor was instructing the pastors, saying, *You should stop teaching doctrine, because doctrine divides the church*!

He appeared to have forgotten that the Word witnesses to the Spirit and the Spirit witnesses to the Word; that without the Word it is hard to judge whether or not the Spirit is genuine. He also did not seem to remember that the brethren are exposed to the false Holy Spirit when there is no doctrinal instruction. To my

13

amazement, the head pastor was not only emphasizing the ministry of the Spirit, he was using our doctrine, the Doctrine of Christ, as an example of why pastors should not teach doctrine. In addition, he made his point so quickly, that the words, *doctrine divides,* was almost subliminal. The pastors did not realize that an ungodly seed had been planted in their mind.

I saw an animal in his eyes, and the Christ in me challenged this man. He spoke to the head pastor in the Spirit, telling him to *turn the meeting over*. This scenario was coming up in my mind, but I had no idea that these thoughts were coming from Christ Jesus within me.

I spoke to him silently in the Spirit, saying, *A greater than you is here!* I was referring to the Christ in me. *Turn the meeting over!* Up to that point, the man had smiled and been kind. But from that moment forward he was absolutely hostile towards me, and would not look me directly in the eye. He must have heard the command on some level, but I doubt that he took it seriously, if he did hear it. Of course, he did not turn the meeting over, and I do not think that the Lord expected him to, but he was surely tested.

VIII.

FALSE TEACHERS

Both Christ and Leviathan, the pride of man, are speaking to everyone that exercises authority in the Church, saying, *let my people go. Turn them over to me.* This was the same message that Jehovah sent to Pharaoh.

Moses and Aaron overshadowed Pharaoh's carnal mind, and in the same manner, the first-fruit Sons will influence the five-fold ministry to turn the people over to Christ Jesus when He appears to them. We have to get the people out of their hands! We will not do anything in our flesh, but through Christ Jesus, the five-fold ministry will have to let the people go. This Pharisaic five-fold ministry will not enter in themselves, and will not allow the people to enter in either. They are the modern day Pharisees.

There is no way that the average person can overcome their leaders to study a doctrine like this on their own, because all that they think about is living in peace, taking care of their kids and family, working and being healthy. They are scared out of their minds to deviate from the norm.

IX.

JUDGMENT

There is a big shaking coming to the Church. Everyone is waiting for Christ to stand up to equip the people to dominate their fallen nature. The Church leaders claim to be God's five-fold ministry sent to equip the people to do just that, but they are not who they say they are. They are natural men led by their fallen nature. Deception is coming, and the Church must leave Egypt to escape it.

This is the Serpent's world. It has taken her 15 billion years to bring forth the intelligent life that she fully intends to possess and to reveal herself through. It is the Serpent's plan to populate the planet with the human race, and live through all the people that she chooses to marry.

X.

AFTER PHYSICAL DEATH

The following awesome word concerning this was revealed in LEM Message #411, *The Two Witnesses Revisited.*

After the first sons stand up, it will take about 1500 years for the Lord to convert mankind into His image. The people who are not converted will go about their normal lives during this time, until the end, when the world is rolled up like a scroll, and goes out like a light.

We could be here in the flesh for a long time, until every human being is converted into Christ. The difference between our doctrine, the Doctrine of Christ, and the Doctrine of Ultimate Reconciliation, is the fate of the personality and the body. In the event that the body and the personality die before immortality is imparted to them, the Christ being formed within that person dies also. None of them will be resurrected. Immortality of the body can only be imparted to conscious human beings, in the flesh. Dead carcasses will not be dug up from under the ground and resurrected. Immortality in the flesh means spiritual ascension to the tenth level of consciousness, which is as high as you can go, and still be in your body.

We will be in the earth for many years until every human being who exists at that time is converted into Christ. We will accomplish this by going from man to man, an individual at a time, helping him with the experience that restores the mind of God. Many will live out their lives and die a natural death, while others will experience ascension into immortality.

The soul incarnates from generation to generation. The soul of a man, who lives out his life and dies without the seed of Christ, migrates into that man's children, or closest relative, and someone in a future generation will be converted into Christ. This process could take a very long time, and lines up exactly with the theory of Quantum Mechanics.

XI.

ULTIMATE RECONCILIATION

I recently read an article in the **New York Times** about the end of our planet, and what the earth will be like at that time. The theory of Quantum Mechanics says that the earth had a beginning, and that one day it will come to an end. No one is going to be in pain, tortured or burned up. The earth will go out like a light, and no one will know what hit them. The scientists say that this will not happen for a trillion years.

I said to the Lord, This is really heavy for my finite mind. Is it true that we are going to be around for a trillion years in the flesh, until every soul returns to God? This is a very awesome thing to say to a carnal human being like me. I have an excitement in my spirit, though, because I believe that the basic theory is true, but we might not be understanding it correctly, especially about the number of years, or being in the flesh all that time.

At some point the Lord will have recovered all of His souls and roll up the world, and that will be the end of it. He will not stop until all the souls are returned to Him, because He owns them all. This is the truth behind the Doctrine of Ultimate Reconciliation. Personalities that lived in the past will not be resurrected, because once a personality dies, it is dead. Personalities and physical bodies experience only one lifetime, unless they are joined to Christ Jesus and go on to immortality through Him.

Evolution is real. Everything that the scientists say is real, except that it is not true of Elohim's work. Evolution is the work of the Serpent.

XII.

THE MIND OF CHRIST

Of all the revelations that God has given me, I do not remember ever being so excited in my spirit about these new important revelations. We have received three within 24 to 48 hours:

- The teaching about evolution.
- The teaching that mankind in the earth must reflect righteous Adam, the heavenly man.
- The revelation that the Lord will not give up until every soul is returned to Him.

This means that we are really close to the mind of Christ being completed within us. We are waiting for the mind of Christ in us to come into full agreement with the Lord Jesus Christ, the One Who completes us. We will stand when Adam in the earth is in full agreement with Righteous Adam in heaven. When we get the doctrine straight, Christ will stand up in us and every soul will be reconciled to God.

We must be in the body to teach the people who believe that they will see their dead relatives again. The truth is that the personality is not saved unless it is joined to Christ Jesus. The man that Christ rises from the dead in, will have his personality preserved in Christ Jesus.

If you were to reach your maturity at 10 years of age, you would spend the rest of your life in that ten year-old personality. I am radically different now than when I was 20 years old. The person that I was at 20 years old is gone. If I were to go into full stature today, it would not be as the 20 year-old Sheila. It would be as

23

the woman that I am today, who is the sum total of all the experiences of the maturing stages of my personality that no longer exist. A maturing personality can be likened to a ten or 20 year-old. Each year of a person's life is a temporary experience that grew the person up, and no longer exists. All of the previous personalities have been swallowed up into the one personality that is appearing at the present time.

XIII.

A SPIRITUAL MAN

We are here as representatives of Christ Jesus to educate the people of God about their potential spirituality in Christ Jesus. Jesus' personality was preserved. He is still a man, but He is very different now from the man He was in the days of His flesh. He is a spiritual man.

There are two men that I know of who were glorified: Elijah and Jesus, but only Jesus became a spiritual man. The spirit of Elijah raised Adam in Jesus from the dead, and now the Spirit of Jesus Christ is raising Adam in the Israel of God from the dead. Are Elijah and Jesus up in heaven as distinct individuals? Is Elijah swallowed up into Jesus? Is Elijah, as well as Jesus, a saviour? I do not know. What I do know, because the Scripture says it, is that Jehovah is the Saviour, and Jesus is the Saviour of the body. The truth is good and I will understand it when I mature to the point of understanding. He wants me to understand more than I want to understand. When we see clearly, and when there is no more evil between us, we shall be like Him.

Jesus is the Truth. Our carnal mind is the evil that stands between us. When our carnal mind is completely under the feet of Christ Jesus, we shall see Him face to face. He is the Truth. At that time, we shall have all the Truth!

XIV.

IMMORTALS

There is such an excitement in me! I think the time is close. Look at the signs and the condition of the world. It is obvious that it is all coming together. It cannot be much longer.

There is a whole world that exists in the second stage of the Fall, where the immortals are. It is in another dimension. They are superior beings, spiritually stronger than we are. We have descended to the third stage of the fall. They will never descend into the third stage.

The immortals are piercing into this world to dominate all humanity. The veil that separates the beings in the second stage of the Fall from the beings in the third stage is dissolving. They are coming through, and they are strong enough to enslave mortal humanity. But they cannot enslave Christ Jesus, who will defeat them.

Gen 6:2

> [2] THAT THE SONS OF GOD SAW THE DAUGHTERS OF MEN THAT THEY WERE FAIR; AND THEY TOOK THEM WIVES OF ALL WHICH THEY CHOSE. **KJV**

Only the people that Christ is appearing in will be able to fight them off. Some that do not have Christ will be protected, but there will be many, including Christians, who will be possessed and destroyed. We have a crisis on our hands, and those who cannot see it, are in ignorant bliss.

TABLE OF REFERENCES

ABOUT THE AUTHOR

SHEILA R. VITALE

Sheila R. Vitale is the Spiritual Leader, Founding Teacher, and Pastor of *Living Epistles Ministries (LEM)*. She moves in the offices of Teacher of Apostolic Doctrine, Prophet, Evangelist and Pastor, has an international following, and has been expounding on the Scripture through a unique spiritual lens for nearly three decades.

She has written more than 50 books based on the Old and New Testaments including *Ephraim, Man of the Earth and The Eagle Ascended (OT), and Salvation* and *Not Without Blood (NT)*. She has also rendered original spiritual interpretations of Biblical texts such as *The Woman in The Well (John, Chapter 4)* and *First Corinthians, Chapter 11*. Her unique, Multi-Part Message style is seen in *LEM* Serial Messages such as *A Place Teeming With Life* (9 Parts) and *Quantum Mechanics in Creation* (18 Parts). Each Part of a Multi-Part Message Series can also be enjoyed as a complete and independent study. In addition, she has defined, explained, illustrated and demonstrated hundreds of spiritual principles throughout more than 1,000 *LEM* Lectures.

Her signature work, however, is the three volumes of *The Alternate Translation Bible (ATB): The Alternate Translation of The Old Testament*, *The Alternate Translation of The New Testament* and *The Alternate Translation of the Book of Revelation*. *The Alternate Translation Bible* is a work in progress (*The ATB Project*). Accordingly, additional spiritual interpretations of both whole and partial Chapters are added from time to time, as they are rendered. The most up-to-date versions of *The ATB Project* may be found online at *The LEM Website (LivingEpistles.org)*. *The ATB* is a *spiritual interpretation* of the Scripture and is not intended to replace traditional translations.

She also analyzed the Greek text of *The Book of Revelation* and preached extensively on it in the early years of *The ATB Project.* During that time she produced 197 distinct *Message Parts*, under 29 specific *Message Titles*, all of which deal with *The Book of Revelation. Also, many* of her books such as, *Adam and The Two Judgments* and *A Study in Unconscious Mind Control*, have been translated into Spanish, as well as *The Book of Revelation.*

Pastor Vitale is an illustrator of spiritual principles, a researcher, a translator and a reviewer of the Modern Social Trends of Family and Culture, as they are revealed through TV programs (*The Sopranos),* movies (*The Matrix* and *The Edge of Tomorrow)* and plays (*Wicked).* She also writes for the *LEM Blog.*

She travels domestically, as well as internationally, preaching and teaching Judeo-Christian Spiritual Philosophy, and has donated Audio Libraries of her Lectures to other ministries in Africa, Asia, Europe and North America,

Pastor Vitale serves *LEM* in a range of spiritual, educational, and administrative functions from *The Selden Centre*, *LEM* headquarters in Selden, New York. She is also a philanthropic individual who supports the *Lighthouse Mission (Patchogue, NY) and HGM – Mission of Hope – Haiti, and other* charitable organizations. She also supports community services such as the *Terryville Fire Department.*

In her spare time, Pastor Vitale enjoys watching movies, attending plays and partaking of cuisines from different cultures. An avid traveler, she has visited several countries in Europe and Africa as well as many cities in the United States.

BEGINNINGS, INSPIRATION AND CALLING

Pastor Vitale began her spiritual journey as a child when her Jewish mother enrolled her in the Hebrew school of an Orthodox synagogue. She experienced the Spirit of God for the first time there in such a profound way that she wept. But after that, when she was only eleven years old, she became very ill and was taken to Mount Sinai Hospital in New York City. She almost died there and has battled with life-threatening health issues ever since. Nevertheless, a deep longing for God continued to pursue her until several years later when she desperately wanted to attend Yeshiva (Jewish high school), but could not. Her secular parents approved of her choice, but could not afford the tuition.

Much later, after years of searching, she once again experienced the Spirit that had brought her to tears in the synagogue of her youth, but this time it was at *Gospel Revivals Ministries,* a Pentecostal church where Deliverance Ministry was emphasized. She had a desire to understand the Bible since she was a child, but Scripture was difficult for her and she struggled with the text. Nevertheless, she read one Chapter of the Bible every day until, one day, *her spiritual eyes opened* and she saw an angel holding a little book.

After that, she attended as many as five teaching services each week for about seven years, the latter part of which she edited *Pastor Holzhauser's* books. But several more years had to pass before *the eyes of her understanding opened even further* and she began to receive *Revelation Knowledge of the Scripture.* She understood at that time that the angel she had seen was the angel of Revelation 10:8.

After about seven years of learning *Deliverance Ministry* and *The Doctrine of Sonship (Bill Britton)* from *Pastor Holzhauser,* she studied the Bible independently under the influence and direction of the Holy Spirit.

In **1998** she began teaching Apostolic Doctrine.

In **1990** she spent three months in Stony Brook Hospital where she recovered from an incurable disease, defeating premature death, once again, and went on to resume teaching and managing *LEM.*

In **1992** she journeyed to Africa for the first time, where she was called to the office of Evangelist.

In the **mid-1990s,** she began to Pastor in addition to being a Teacher of Apostolic Doctrine, a Prophet and an Evangelist, thus, satisfying all five offices of *The Ministry of the Lord Jesus Christ to His Church.*

LIVING EPISTLES MINISTRIES

Pastor Vitale was happy fellowshipping at *Gospel Revivals Ministries* but, eventually, she desired a deeper and more spiritual understanding of the Word of God. One day, after crying out to Jesus about her need, she was amazed to hear Him ask her if she would teach. Her initial response was that she did not see how it would be possible since she was already working a full-time job, despite her poor health. But after the Lord asked her for a second and then a third time, she reluctantly agreed, believing that He would empower her to do the job. Shortly thereafter, in the latter part of 1987, she began to teach her own brand of Judeo-Christian Spiritual Philosophy.

The Lord Jesus Christ named the work *Living Epistles Ministries* in 1988.

The first *LEM* meetings were casual and spontaneous gatherings of friends and fellow deliverance workers in Pastor Vitale's home. After that, they were held in the business office of one of the brethren. Pastor Vitale delivered her first formal message entitled *The Truth About Witchcraft in January of 1988*, followed by *The Seduction of Eve* in April of the same year. After that, she prepared and taught weekly messages including *Signs of Apostleship* and *Lazarus & The Rich Man. The meetings eventually* increased to two and then three each week.

Sometime after that, she learned that the Lord Jesus Christ was revealing spiritual principles from the Hebrew text of the Old Testament through her teachings, and she used those spiritual principles to begin to unlock the mysteries of the New Testament, as well. Today she understands that the Scripture is a spiritual document that must be spiritually discerned if it is to be understood

34

correctly, and calls that spiritual understanding ***The Doctrine of Christ****.*

LEM publishes a wide range of material, including books, e-books, spiritual interpretations of the Scripture and transcripts of many of Pastor Vitale's Lectures and on-line meetings, all of which, as well as the entire *Alternate Translation Bible,* may be viewed free of charge on the *LEM* website (*LivingEpistles.org*). She also has an *Author's Website* where all of her books, as well as several photographs of herself and a short biography are displayed (Amazon.com/author/SheilaVitale). Paperback and digital versions of *LEM* books may be purchased through *Amazon, Google Books* and *Barnes & Noble.*

LEM provides free video livestreams through YouTube and other Internet Platforms . . .

@LivingEpistlesMinistries (2016 – Sept. 2022)
@LivingEpistlesMinistriesLEM (Oct. 2022 – Ongoing)
@LivingEpistlesMinistries (LEM disciples)

. . . as well as two channels of ***Shortclips*** where short, focused messages of about 15 minutes each are posted:

@shortclipsbysheilar.vitale3334 (2016 – Sept. 2022)
@ShortClips-SheilaVitale (Oct. 2022 – Ongoing)

LEM donates a significant percentage of its income to other Christian ministries and organizations that advocate for Christian values and defend the United States Constitution.

PASTOR VITALE TODAY

Today Pastor Vitale continues to dedicate her life to teaching the spiritual principles of the Bible and focuses daily on studying, writing and preaching powerful messages from *The Selden Centre,* LEM/CCK's headquarters at Selden, New York.

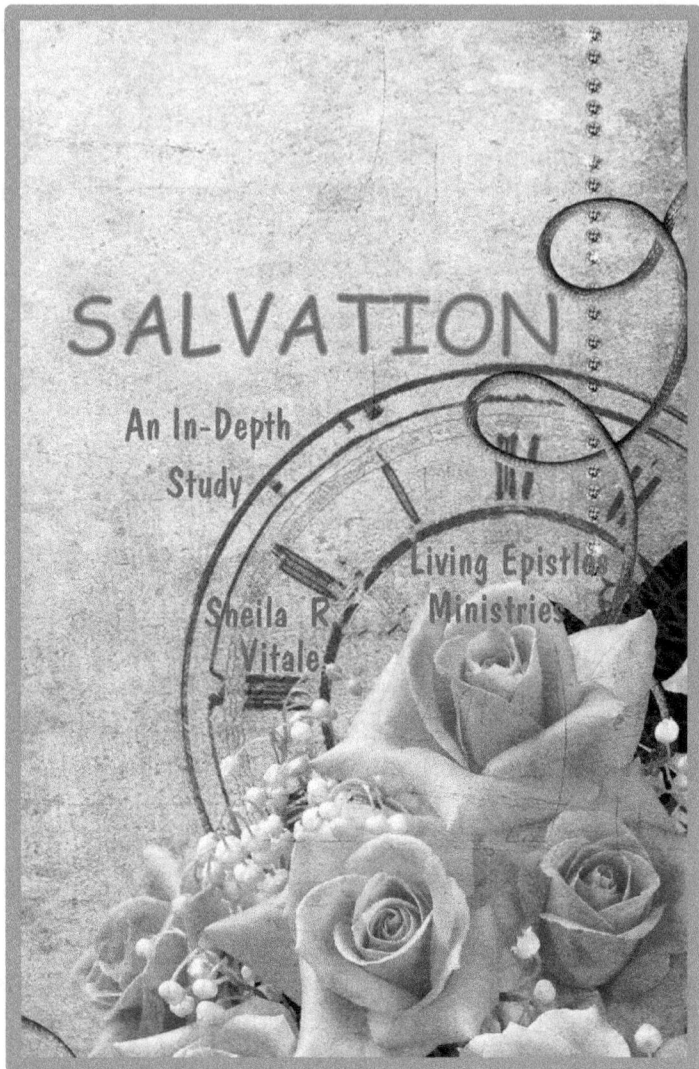

Salvation is an in-depth study which includes Redemption, Sanctification, Adoption and Forgiveness, as well as some insight into Salvation for Israel.

THE TRUTH ABOUT BAPTISM

A Study in Baptism & Tongues

Sheila R. Vitale
Living Epistles Ministries

The Truth About Baptism is a study in Baptism and Tongues. Subtopics include, Prophecy, The Gospel of the Cross vs. the Gospel of Perfection, and the Spirit of Antichrist

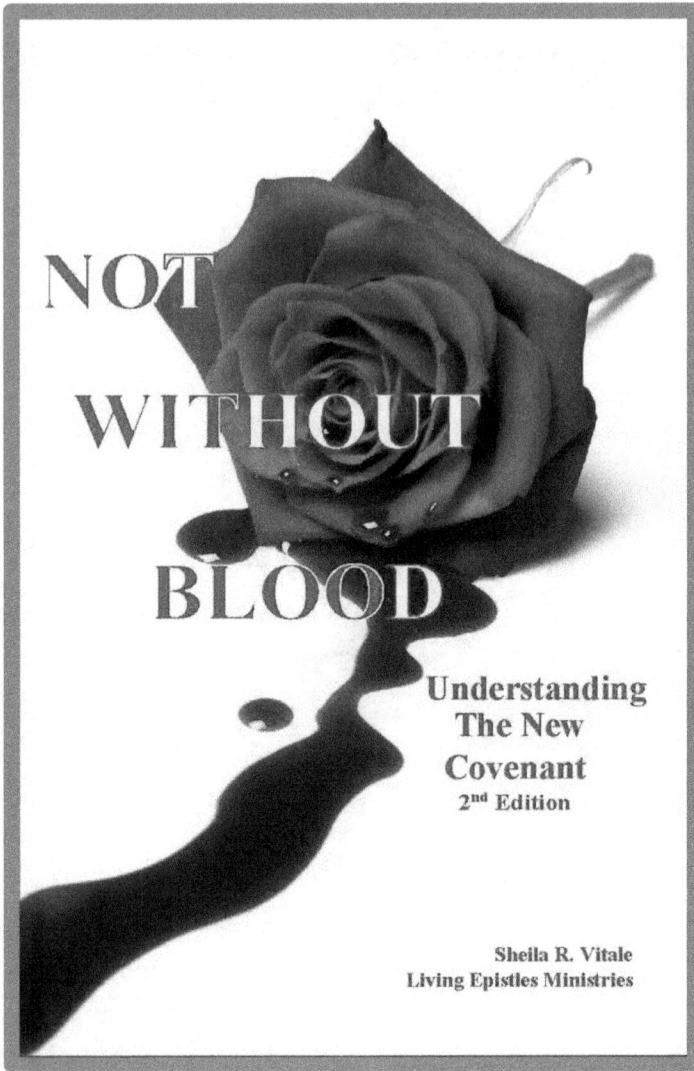

Not Without Blood explains that Jesus' sacrifice gained access to the throne of God for all mankind, but that each individual must offer up his own sin nature in exchange for Jesus' righteousness nature.

Living Epistles Ministries
Sheila R. Vitale
Pastor, Teacher & Founder
Judeo-Christian Spiritual Philosophy
PO Box 562, Port Jefferson Station, New York 11776, USA
LivingEpistles.org
or
Books@LivingEpistles.org

www.ingramcontent.com/pod-product-compliance
Lightning Source LLC
La Vergne TN
LVHW051204080426
835508LV00021B/2794